What Am I?

What Kind of BUG AM I?

Taylor Farley

TABLE OF CONTENTS

A Crabtree Seedlings Book

What Kind of Bug Am I?

I am red with black spots.

What kind of bug am I?

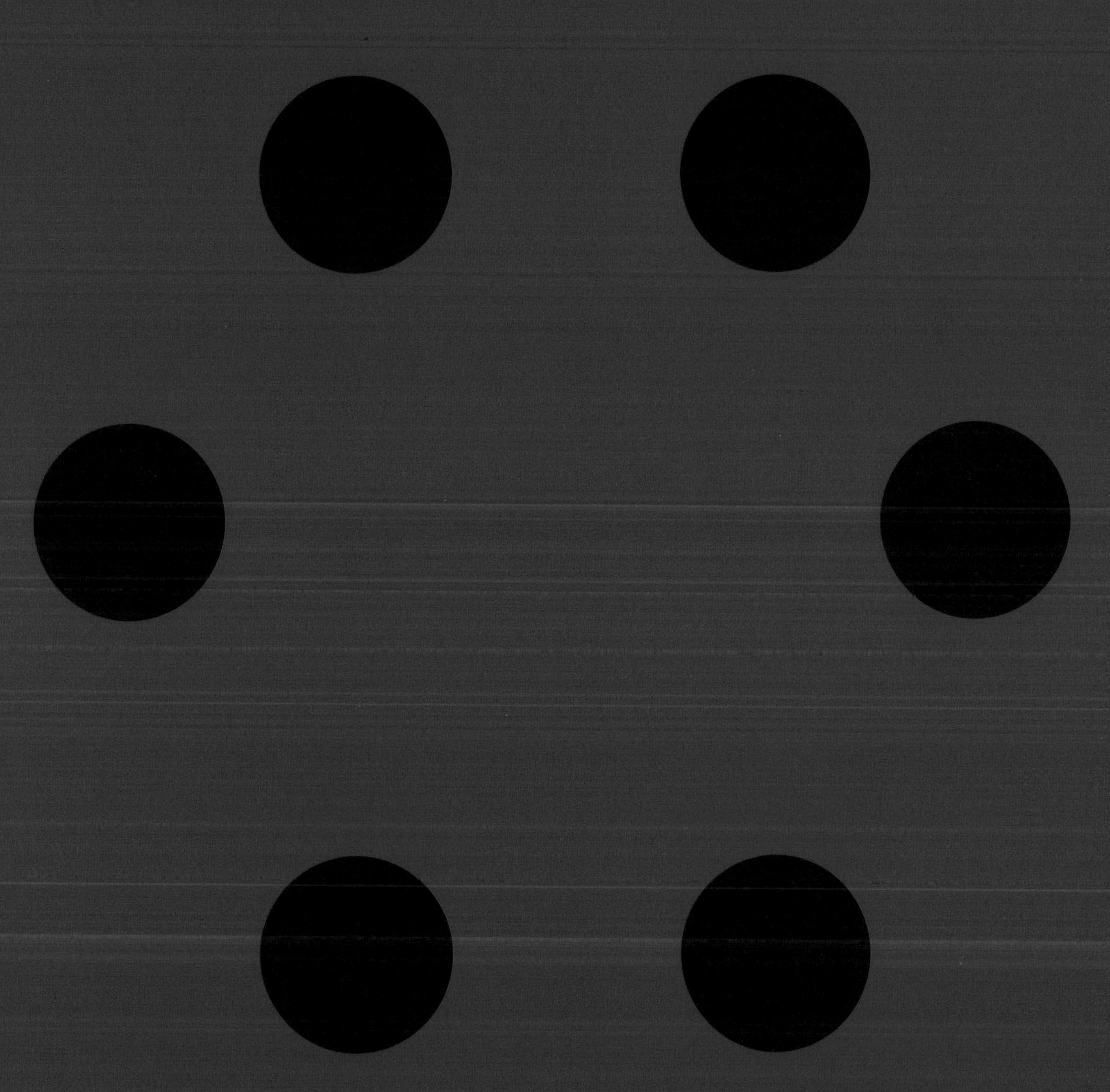

A ladybug

I have black stripes and yellow stripes.

What kind of bug am I?

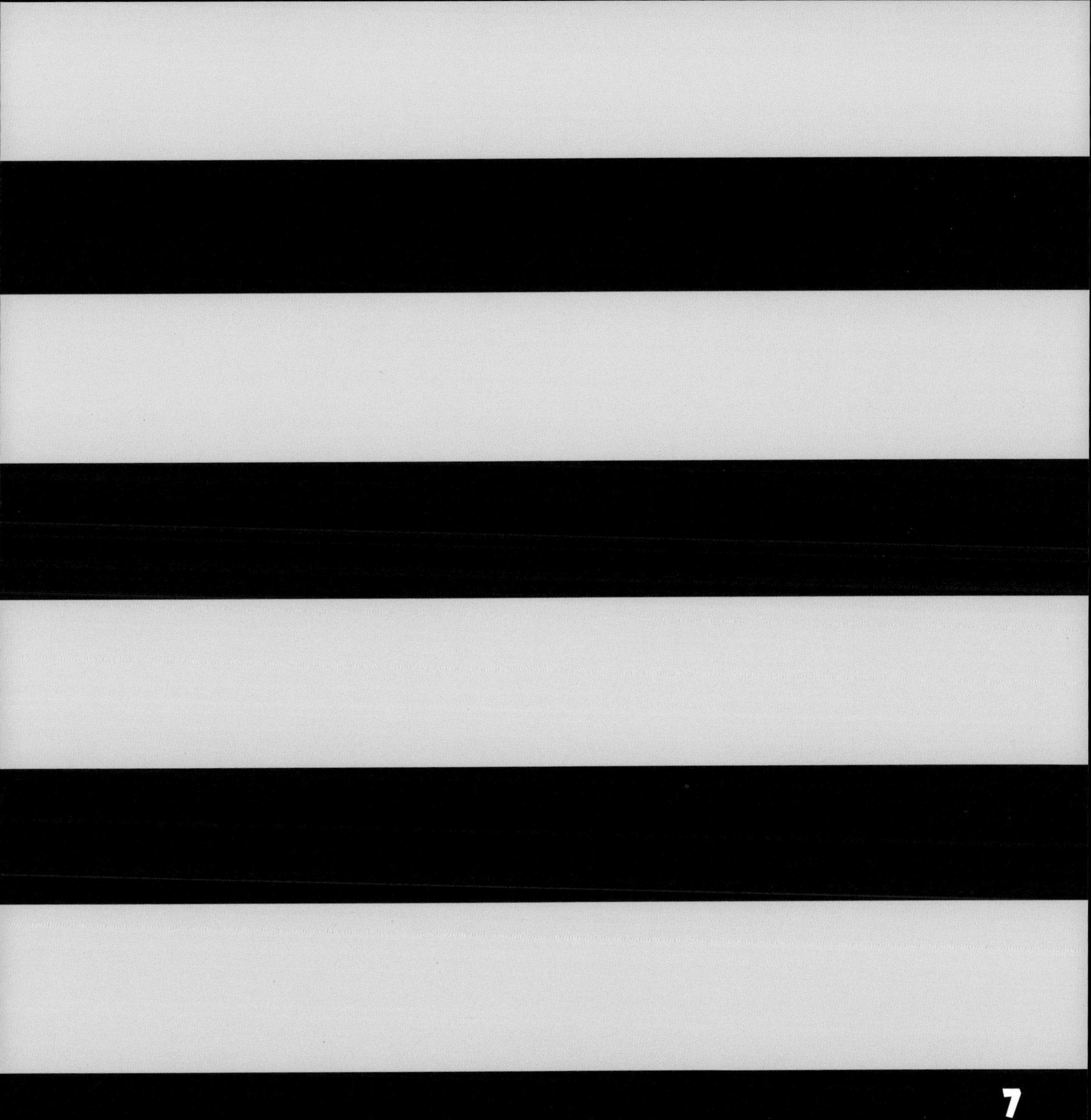

A bee

I have a hairy body
and lots of legs.

What kind of bug am I?

A caterpillar

I am green all over
and can jump very high.

What kind of bug am I?

A grasshopper

I buzz like a bee
and like to eat poop!

What kind of bug am I?

A fly

Glossary

bee (BEE): Bees are important because they spread pollen from plant to plant. Without bees, many kinds of plants would not grow.

caterpillar (KAT-ur-pil-ur): At the right time, a caterpillar will form a chrysalis or a cocoon and then change into a butterfly or a moth.

fly (FLYE): A fly does not have teeth. It can only eat liquids. It turns solid food into liquid by spitting on it.

grasshopper (GRASS-hop-ur): A grasshopper can hear sounds through a thin layer of skin on its belly.

ladybug (LAY-dee-buhg): A ladybug is a kind of beetle. Its bright red color warns other bugs and animals to stay away.

Index

What Is a Bug?
"Bug" is often used to describe all insects. In fact, bugs are special because they have extra wings and a mouthpart shaped like a straw for sucking. That means all of the "bugs" in this book are actually insects, not true bugs.

School-to-Home Support for Caregivers and Teachers

This book helps children grow by letting them practice reading. Here are a few guiding questions to help the reader build his or her comprehension skills. Possible answers appear here in red.

Before Reading

- **What do I think this book is about?** I think this book is about different kinds of bugs. I think this book is about how scary some bugs are.
- **What do I want to learn about this topic?** I want to learn more about bugs that sting people. I want to learn about the good things that bugs do to help people.

During Reading

- **I wonder why...** I wonder why caterpillars have so many legs. I wonder why a fly likes to eat poop.
- **What have I learned so far?** I have learned that a grasshopper is all green. I have learned that an insect has six legs.

After Reading

- **What details did I learn about this topic?** I have learned that bees spread pollen from plant to plant. I have learned that a fly does not have teeth.
- **Read the book again and look for the glossary words.** I see the word *caterpillar* on page 12, and the word *grasshopper* on page 17. The other glossary words are found on pages 22 and 23.

Library and Archives Canada Cataloguing in Publication

CIP available at Library and Archives Canada

Library of Congress Cataloging-in-Publication Data

CIP available at Library of Congress

Crabtree Publishing Company
www.crabtreebooks.com 1-800-387-7650

Written by: Taylor Farley
Print coordinator: Katherine Berti

Print book version produced jointly with Blue Door Education in 2023

Printed in the U.S.A./072022/CG20220201

PHOTO CREDITS:
ladybug © Gerisima; bee © arcticphotoworks; caterpillar © Alen thien; grasshopper © Ingrid Prats; fly eyes © Denis Vesely; fly © Worraket.
All photos from Shutterstock.com

Published in the United States
Crabtree Publishing
347 Fifth Ave.
Suite 1402-145
New York, NY 10016

Published in Canada
Crabtree Publishing
616 Welland Ave.
St. Catharines, Ontario
L2M 5V6